COOKING THE
TURKISH
WAY

Lerner Publications Company thanks our expert consultant Nurçay Türkoğlu for her contributions to this book.

Lerner Publications Company
A division of Lerner Publishing Group
241 First Avenue North
Minneapolis, MN 55401 U.S.A.

Website address: www.lernerbooks.com

Library of Congress Cataloging-in-Publication Data

Cornell, Kari A.
    Cooking the Turkish way / Kari A. Cornell and Nurcay Turkoglu.
        p.   cm. — (Easy menu ethnic cookbooks)
    Summary: An introduction to cooking in Turkey, featuring such recipes as spinach-filled Anatolian flat bread, lamb kebabs, and baklava. Also includes information on the history, geography, customs, and people of this partly European and partly Asian country.
    ISBN: 0–8225–4123–8 (lib. bdg. : alk. paper)
    1. Cookery, Turkish—Juvenile literature. 2. Turkey—Social life and customs—Juvenile literature. 3. Low-fat diet—Recipes—Juvenile literature. 4. Vegetarian cookery—Juvenile literature. [1. Cookery, Turkey. 2. Turkey—Social life and customs.] I. Turkoglu, Nurcay. II. Title.
TX725.T8C67 2004
641.59561—dc22   2003016543

Manufactured in the United States of America
1 2 3 4 5 6 – JR – 09 08 07 06 05 04

COOKING

culturally authentic foods

THE

including low-fat and

TURKISH

vegetarian recipes

WAY

Kari Cornell and Nurçay Türkoğlu

Lerner Publications Company • Minneapolis

Contents

Introduction

If you were to travel through Turkey, sampling food along the way, you would be savoring a unique and rich cuisine that has been ranked among some of the best cooking in the world. And you would be tasting a bit of Turkish history. Along the coast of the Aegean Sea, for example, olives and seafood—foods commonly associated with Greek cuisine—are popular. Around 900 B.C., Greeks inhabited this coast, where they established the settlements of Ephesus, Miletus, and Troy. The newcomers brought along the traditions of their homeland, including favorite recipes.

Head eastward along the Mediterranean Sea and food begins to take on the flavors of the Middle East. Dishes such as kebabs (chunks of lamb, beef, or chicken roasted on skewers), hummus (pureed chickpeas, sesame paste, and garlic dip), kısır (small patties made from bulgur, parsley, and spicy tomato paste), and muhammara (a spicy red pepper and nut spread) become more prominent. During the time of the Turkish Ottoman Empire (1453–1909), Turks ruled all or parts of modern-day Middle Eastern countries such as Iraq, Syria, Saudi Arabia, and Egypt. They also ruled parts of many other countries, such as Russia and Hungary.

A Turkish holiday meal might include generous slices of a baked meat and cheese pie. (Recipe on pages 68–69.)

7

But it was in İstanbul, the former center of the Ottoman Empire, where the recipes traditionally thought of as Turkish originated. In the vast kitchens of the Topkapı Palace, cooks dreamed up new dishes in hopes of delighting the sultan, the great ruler of the empire. Ottoman cooks were fortunate to have a wealth of fresh vegetables, fruits, nuts, and meats from which to create the most enticing foods. Traders from China and India traveled through the Ottoman Empire on a network of trade routes, bringing spices such as cinnamon, nutmeg, allspice, cloves, and cumin, many of which found their way into traditional Ottoman recipes. Eventually these recipes became popular throughout the empire, and they remain favorites among Turks in modern times.

In this book, we've included a sampling of recipes that represent the vast range of Turkish cuisine. We hope that you enjoy them all. As Turkish cooks say to their guests, "Afiyet olsun!" This expression, which means "Enjoy your meal," is used both before and after dinner. After indulging in these fine dishes, express your appreciation for food prepared by somebody else by saying *"Elinize saglik!"* ("May God give health to your hands!")

The Land and Its People

Turkey (Türkiye in Turkish) is known as the place where East meets West and North meets South, both physically and in spirit. Because of its strategic location where the continents of Asia and Europe almost touch, Turkey has been important in world history and is the birthplace of many great civilizations.

Although most of Turkey lies on the Asian continent in an area known as Anatolia, the Turkish region known as Thrace is firmly planted on European soil. The Bosporus Strait, a busy waterway that connects the Black Sea in the north to the Sea of Marmara in the south, marks the boundary between the two continents. The strait also divides İstanbul, Turkey's largest city. At different times, İstanbul was the capital of three great empires—Roman, Byzantine, and Ottoman. Since 1920 Ankara, a city in Central Anatolia, has been the capital of the Turkish Republic.

Turkey is one of the largest countries in Europe and the Middle East. With a land area of 309,000 square miles, it is slightly smaller than Texas and Louisiana combined. The country shares its western border with Greece, Bulgaria, and the Aegean Sea. The Republic of Georgia, Armenia, and Iran flank Turkey on the east, while Iraq, Syria, and the Mediterranean Sea form Turkey's southern border. The Black Sea defines Turkey's northern edge.

The area along the Black Sea receives more rain than does any other part of the country. The Pontic Mountains rim this coastal area and form a natural barrier, separating this region from the rest of Turkey. The thick forests that cover the mountains provide lumber for the boat-building industry, an age-old tradition. Tea plants, whose leaves are dried and crushed to make the Turks' favorite drink, also flourish on these hillsides. In the winter months, the fishing crews that cast into the waves off the coast catch primarily anchovies (several varieties of small fish).

The terrain just inland from the rugged, dry Aegean coast is some of the most fertile land in Turkey. Olives, grapes, figs, oranges, tangerines, and artichokes flourish in the sunny, warm climate that characterizes this region. Ancient Greek and Roman ruins along this coast make it a popular destination for visitors.

To the south and east, the waves of the Mediterranean roll into shore. Along this coast, the Taurus Mountains spike the landscape, breaking up only between the seaside resort towns of Antalya and Alanya. Off the coast of Antalya, fishing crews reel in fish such as red sea bream, bluefish, red mullet, and bonito. Between these two cities and the city of Adana to the east stretches a plain where cotton farms predominate. The more tropical climate near Adana provides perfect growing conditions for watermelons, oranges, mandarins, and bananas. Farmers in this region have also begun to cultivate mangoes, guavas, kiwis, papayas, and avocados.

In Turkey's interior, goats and sheep graze along the mountains and grasslands of the Central Plateau. A region called Cappadocia is marked by soft volcanic rock that has been eroded over the centuries to create unique land formations called fairy chimneys. Farther east, extensive irrigation systems have transformed the once-barren land into a rich agricultural area. Diyarbakir is famous for its watermelons. Other crops that prosper in this area include wheat, lentils, chickpeas, onions, sugarcane, peppers, spinach, pistachios, walnuts, pomegranates, and plums.

Approximately 70 million people live in modern Turkey, and most of them are ethnic Turks. The Turkic people were originally members of a number of different nomadic groups from Central Asia. In the eleventh century A.D., the Mongols, a powerful Central Asian group, began forcing people out of the area, and many Turks fled to Anatolia. One Turkic group established the powerful Seljuk Empire in 1037. The Seljuks brought to Anatolia the Islamic faith, a

In the 1400s, Ottoman sultan Mehmed the Conqueror started building the majestic Topkapi Palace in İstanbul.

religion established on the Arabian Peninsula in the seventh century A.D. that they had recently come into contact with. During the thirteenth century, other groups of Turks headed into areas along the Sea of Marmara and the Aegean coast. One of these groups formed the beginnings of the Ottoman Empire. Replacing the Christianity of the Roman and Byzantine eras, Islam became the predominant religion. Although present-day Turkey is a secular (nonreligious) state, 99 percent of the population is Sunni Muslim, followers of a branch of Islam.

The largest minority ethnic group in Turkey is the Kurds. Kurds are spread out across Turkey, Iran, Iraq, Syria, and southern regions of the former Soviet Union. Between 10 and 12 million Kurds live in Turkey, mostly in the southeastern part of the country. Many Armenians—people from the country of Armenia—live in Turkey as well. Most live in İstanbul or around Lake Van in the eastern part of the country. Two Turkish subgroups, the Laz and the Hemşin peoples, live between the Pontic Mountains and the Black Sea and maintain distinct cultures and traditions.

Turkey is also home to a small Jewish community. The majority of Turkish Jews are descendants of those who fled to Turkey from Spain in the 1500s during the Spanish Inquisition (a time when the Catholic Church imprisoned, tortured, and killed non-Catholics). Many settled in the Turkish cities of İstanbul, Ankara, İzmir, and Bursa.

Regional Cooking

The history of food in Anatolia stretches back to advanced agricultural civilizations such as the Hittites, who lived in the region in 7000 to 6000 B.C. Some foods—such as eggplant, tomatoes, kebabs, and bread—are everywhere in Turkey. But the way these foods are prepared varies from region to region, depending upon local preferences and additional ingredients available.

Turkey is divided into seven climate regions, each of which makes its own contributions to the country's cuisine. The Marmara region includes İstanbul and the communities surrounding the Sea of Marmara. This small swath of land, where the cultures of Europe and Asia blend, is the place to savor favorite Turkish or international foods. Marmara is known for its Ottoman specialties, including fried, baked, stuffed, or roasted eggplant; kebabs; and Turkish delight, a popular candy. Seafood, such as the famous fish sandwiches sold on the banks of the Bosporus in İstanbul and the region's fried or stuffed mussels, is very popular. The city of Bursa, located on the southern shore of the Sea of Marmara, is home to the *döner kebap*, a specialty kebab made from lamb, beef, or chicken. The meat, cut from the skewer in thin slices, is served on pita bread (a traditional flat bread) with yogurt and tomato sauce.

The Aegean region is known for its squid, which cooks typically fry in a light batter to make a dish called calamari. Fresh fish and shellfish, including stuffed mussels, are also particularly good here. Olives, oranges, artichokes, and figs are just a few of the fresh fruits and vegetables that grow locally.

Along the Mediterranean, several varieties of grilled fresh fish make savory main courses. *Tandır kebab*, skewered meat cooked in a clay oven, is a specialty in Antalya. In Alanya to the east, *kuzu kaburga dolmasi*, lamb ribs stuffed with nuts, shredded meat, rice, and vegetables, is a favorite local dish. This city is also famous for its jams. Mixed in with the usual jars of strawberry, sour cherry, and apricot varieties are preserves made from watermelons, carrots, pumpkins, roses, and even eggplants. The kebabs served in Adana—called *Adana kebap*—are spicier than those served in western Turkey, reflecting the Arabic influence of nearby Syria. To prepare Adana kebap, ground lamb is mixed with onion, paprika, and parsley, shaped into meatballs, skewered, and grilled.

North of the Mediterranean coast lies the region of Central Anatolia. Dishes based on pasta, pastry, or bread are especially popular in this part of the country. *Gözleme*, for example, can be savored throughout Anatolia. This pancake of phyllo dough (flaky pastry) is layered with spinach, onion, cheese, or other filling. It is folded, grilled, and served like a sandwich. To make *börek*, another regional specialty, cooks layer phyllo dough with meat or spinach in a clay pot (*tandır*) and bake until it is golden brown. Kayseri, a town in the Cappadocia region of Central Anatolia, is famous for *pastirma*, a preserved meat, and for *mantı*, tiny pasta dumplings stuffed with ground vegetables, lamb, or beef, and topped with a garlic-flavored yogurt sauce.

In Southeastern Anatolia, Syrian influence is strong. Here the food is spicy, and bulgur wheat replaces the rice that's commonly served alongside main dishes throughout the rest of the country. Typical Arab dishes, including hummus, *babaghannush* (mashed baked eggplant mixed with yogurt and garlic), and muhammara are prominent.

Eastern Anatolia has been home to the Kurdish people for centuries. *Kürt köftesi*, a dumpling made from bulgur, chopped onions, and fresh mint, is a traditional Kurdish dish. Van, a city that lies between Lake Van and the Iranian border, is famous for *van otlu*, a sharp, white cheese mixed with bits of grass. Egg dishes, such as *çılbır*—poached eggs served with yogurt—are especially popular in Van. Malatya is known for its sweet and abundant apricots. Many of the dried apricots available in markets across the country come from this region. Malatya's *pestil*, dried apricots that have been mashed and flattened into thin sheets, is famous. Another popular treat is *küme*, pestil layered with nuts and rolled up into a log-shaped treat.

The Eastern Anatolian city of Gaziantep is known for its pistachios and for its syrupy sweet baklava, a flaky dessert made with honey and pistachios or other nuts. Pistachios are included in many local specialties, including *fıstıklı kebap*—spicy, ground meat rolled in crushed pistachios and then cooked—and *künefe*, a rich, gooey dessert consisting of two thin, syrupy layers of dough stuffed with cheese and topped with chopped pistachios.

Along the Black Sea coast, anchovies are popular—so popular that they even make their way into local desserts. *Hamsi tatlısı* is a sweet pastry made from anchovies, flour, eggs, and fruit preserves. The salty fish also flavors more traditional, savory dishes such as pilaf (rice that is sometimes mixed with vegetables and spices) and börek. The Laz people in this area are known throughout Turkey for baking a distinctive corn bread. Their neighbors the Hemşin are famous for making wonderful pastries and puddings. In fact, many of the renowned pudding shops in İstanbul are Hemşin businesses.

Holidays and Festivals

Although Turkey is 99 percent Muslim, many of the country's holidays are secular in nature. Mustafa Kemal, known as Atatürk (Father of the Turks) founded the Turkish Republic in 1920. This revered leader shaped modern Turkey, making it more Westernized and secular than much of the rest of the Muslim world. He made many changes

A boy carries a Turkish flag to celebrate a holiday proclaimed by Atatürk (right).

in Turkey, including replacing Arabic script with the Latin alphabet, introducing a Western-style legal system, and ending religious education in Turkish schools.

In 1923 Atatürk made April 23 National Independence Day. Six years later, Turks observed the first Children's Day on April 23, a tradition that has continued ever since. Children's Day acknowledges the important role children play in the future of all nations. On this day, hundreds of children from throughout the world arrive in Turkey. They stay with families in Turkish homes, sample Turkish foods, and experience Turkish culture. On November 10, the anniversary of Atatürk's death, Turks observe a moment of silence to remember this great leader.

Turks host a number of other festivals throughout the year. Many events, such as the International Film Festival in the spring and the International İstanbul Festival in the summer, attract lovers of art films, opera, ballet, and other performances to İstanbul. Festivals such as the Cappadocia Wine Festival in Ürgüp and the watermelon festival in Diyarbakır celebrate bountiful harvests.

Celebrating New Year's Eve and New Year's Day (January 1) is popular in Turkey. People wish friends and family a happy New Year by sending greeting cards, e-mailing, or telephoning a few weeks before the holiday. It's very common for people to exchange small gifts on

New Year's Day. People celebrate much like they do in the United States, by throwing parties and listening to music. Turks also watch television over the holiday, when local channels typically broadcast their best programs.

For religious Turks, Ramazan—called Ramadan in many other Islamic countries—is the most significant holiday. Ramazan takes place during the ninth month of the Islamic calendar, the holiest time of the year. The holiday commemorates the time when Muhammad, the most important prophet in the Islamic faith, received his first messages from god, called Allah in Islam. During this sacred month, Muslims who are in good health fast by not eating or drinking from sunrise to sunset. (Pregnant women, the elderly, and children do not fast.) To prepare for the daylong fast, people eat a big meal, called *imsak* or *sahur*, before dawn. The meal, which typically consists of soup, bread with jam, olives, pastries, dates, and tea, provides energy for the daylight hours.

Just as the sun is setting, it is a tradition for children to go to the neighborhood bakery to buy freshly baked pita. The children wait in line, holding coins tightly in their fists. The baker gives each child a hot pita wrapped in paper so it doesn't burn their hands. On the way home, children may sneak a bite of the pita.

The muezzin (a Muslim who chants the call to prayer from a mosque, or Islamic house of worship) calls out an end to the fast at sunset. İftariyelik, a snack commonly consisting of dates and olives, satisfies people's hunger until the main meal, called *iftar*, is served. Men traditionally go to the mosque to pray while the women prepare the food. And what a feast it is! Soup, pastirma cooked with eggs, kebabs, börek made with lamb or spinach, pilaf, and vegetables such as green beans and eggplant commonly fill the table. The customary Ramazan dessert is *güllaç*, a mouthwatering pastry made from rice wafers, sweetened milk, rose water, and walnuts.

Three days of celebration, called Şeker Bayramı, end the month-long Ramazan fast. Most religious Turks try to return home to visit family for Şeker Bayramı. In preparation for the holiday, people shake out the carpets, scrub the floors, and dust the furniture, ensuring that everything is in order for visiting family and friends. People dress in their best clothes and feast on sweets such as baklava, *sütlâç* (rice pudding), and *şeker pare* (syrup-topped shortbread cookies). Dried apricots, pistachios, dates, almonds, and savory dishes made from beans and lentils are also part of the Şeker Bayramı feast. *Yuvarlama*, a soup made with chickpea dumplings, is the traditional dish made to celebrate the holiday in Southeastern Anatolia. On Şeker Bayramı, children look forward to more than just the fabulous food—adults traditionally shower them with gifts and candies.

Another widely celebrated holiday in Turkey is Kurban Bayramı, the feast of the sacrifice. Families, even those who are not devout Muslims, celebrate the holiday by having a professional butcher slaughter a sheep for them. Blood from the animal is dabbed on children's foreheads for luck. The family typically keeps some of the meat and donates the rest to the poor.

The Mevlana Festival is an Islamic event that takes place each December in Konya. This is the one time of year when visitors can watch the whirling dervishes—members of a religious sect within Islam—spin in a mesmerizing, age-old dance.

The whirling dervishes' dizzying dance dates back to the thirteenth century.

Before You Begin

Cooking any dish, plain or fancy, is easier and more fun if you are familiar with its ingredients. The Turkish dishes in this book make use of some ingredients you may not know. You should also be familiar with the special terms that will be used in these recipes. Therefore, before you start cooking, study the following "dictionary" of special ingredients and terms very carefully.

Be sure to read through the recipe you want to try from beginning to end. Then you are ready to shop for ingredients and to organize the cookware you will need. Once you have assembled everything, you can begin to cook. It is also important to read "The Careful Cook" before you start. Following these rules will make your cooking experience safe, fun, and easy.

Flat bread makes a satisfying side for an entrée of chicken cooked with rice, tomatoes, bell peppers, and tarragon. (Recipes on pages 64–65 and 46–47.)

The Careful Cook

Whenever you cook, there are certain safety rules you must always keep in mind. Even experienced cooks follow these rules when they are in the kitchen.

- Always wash your hands before handling food. Thoroughly wash all raw vegetables and fruits to remove dirt, chemicals, and insecticides. Wash uncooked poultry, fish, and meat under cold water.
- Use a cutting board when cutting up vegetables and fruits. Don't cut them up in your hand! And be sure to cut in a direction *away* from you and your fingers.
- Long hair or loose clothing can easily catch fire if brought near the burners of a stove. If you have long hair, tie it back before you start cooking.
- Turn all pot handles toward the back of the stove so that you will not catch your sleeves or jewelry on them. This is especially important when younger brothers and sisters are around. They could easily knock off a pot and get burned.
- Always use a pot holder to steady hot pots or to take pans out of the oven. Don't use a wet cloth on a hot pan because the steam it produces could burn you.
- Lift the lid of a steaming pot with the opening away from you so that you will not get burned.
- If you get burned, hold the burn under cold running water. Do not put grease or butter on it. Cold water helps to take the heat out, but grease or butter will only keep it in.
- If grease or cooking oil catches fire, throw baking soda or salt at the bottom of the flame to put it out. (Water will *not* put out a grease fire.) Call for help, and try to turn all the stove burners to "off."

Cooking Utensils

Dutch oven—A heavy pot with a tight-fitting, domed lid that is often used for cooking soups or stews

pastry brush—A small brush with nylon bristles used for coating food with melted butter or other liquids

skewer—A thin metal or wooden rod used to hold small pieces of food for broiling or grilling

strainer—A small wire mesh bowl with attached handle used to separate liquid from solid food

Cooking Terms

beat—To stir rapidly in a circular motion

broil—To cook food under a direct flame

brown—To cook food quickly over high heat so that the surface browns evenly

grate—To cut into tiny pieces by rubbing food against a grater

knead—To work dough by pressing it with the palms, pushing it outward, and then pressing it over on itself

marinate—To soak food in a seasoned liquid in order to add flavor and to tenderize it

mince—To chop food into very small pieces

preheat—To heat an oven before using it

puree—To make food into a paste or thick liquid

sauté—To fry quickly in oil or fat, over high heat, stirring or turning the food to prevent burning

simmer—To cook over low heat in liquid kept just below its boiling point. Bubbles may occasionally rise to the surface.

Special Ingredients

barley—A whole grain that is often used to thicken soups

blanched almonds—Almonds with the thin brown skin removed, available in the baking section of most grocery stores

chickpeas—Legumes that are yellow in color and slightly larger than green peas. Chickpeas (also called garbanzo beans) have a firm texture and mild, nutlike flavor.

coriander—The ground seeds from the cilantro plant, used as seasoning

crushed red pepper—The dried crushed seeds and skin of a hot red pepper, used to season foods

cumin—The seeds of an herb used whole or ground to give food a pungent, slightly hot flavor

currants—Small, seedless raisins used in Mediterranean cooking

eggplant—A vegetable with shiny, purple-black skin and light-colored flesh that is very popular in Turkish cuisine

feta cheese—A soft, crumbly white cheese that is commonly made with goat's or sheep's milk. Feta has a distinctive, salty taste.

fig—A sweet, dried fruit with many tiny seeds. Figs may be eaten plain or used to flavor desserts.

garlic—A bulbous herb with a distinctive flavor used in many dishes. Each bulb can be broken can be broken into small sections called cloves. Before chopping a clove of garlic, remove its papery skin.

nigella seeds—A black, aromatic seed sprinkled on bread and pastries. Nigella seeds (sometimes called black cumin seeds) are available at Middle Eastern grocery stores. If you cannot find them, you can substitute sesame seeds.

olive oil—An oil, made from pressed olives, that is used in cooking and for salad dressing

paprika—Dried, ground sweet red peppers used to flavor or color foods *phyllo dough*—A flaky pastry rolled into paper-thin sheets that are almost transparent. Phyllo dough can be made from scratch or purchased from the frozen foods section of most grocery stores. Allow the dough to thaw in the refrigerator for at least 8 hours before using.

pine nuts—A rich, edible seed that grows on some pine trees

pistachios—A flavorful, light-green nut used to flavor many Turkish desserts. The already-cracked shells of this nut are easy to remove, but look for pre-shelled varieties to save time.

pita bread—Flat, round loaves of unleavened bread. When baked, a puffed pocket of air forms in the center of the bread.

red lentils—Tiny, orange-red legumes used to make soups and spreads in Mediterranean countries

rice flour—A flour made from ground rice and commonly used in desserts

rice wafers—Thin crackers, made from rice flour, that are used in Turkish desserts. Look for them in Middle Eastern markets.

rose water—A liquid distilled from rose petals that is used to flavor many Turkish desserts. Look for rose water at your local grocery store or in Mediterranean markets.

short-grain rice—A variety of rice with thicker grains that cook to a sticky consistency. Short-grain rice is available at your local grocery store or Middle Eastern market.

tarragon—A fragrant herb commonly used to flavor chicken dishes

yeast—An ingredient used in baking that causes dough to rise. Yeast is available in either small, white cakes called compressed yeast or in granular form called active yeast.

yogurt—A common ingredient in Turkish cuisine. To achieve the flavor and thicker consistency of Turkish yogurts, strain plain, nonfat, or low-fat yogurt through cheesecloth to remove extra water.

Healthy and Low-Fat Cooking Tips

Many modern cooks are concerned about preparing healthy, low-fat meals. Fortunately, there are simple ways to reduce the fat content of most dishes without losing flavor. Tips for adapting these recipes are provided here and throughout the book.

To cut fat from recipes, consider using less olive oil than the recipe calls for. Sprinkling a little salt on the vegetables brings out their natural juices, so less oil is needed. It's also a good idea to use a nonstick frying pan if you decide to use less oil than the recipe calls for. Or substitute a low-fat or nonfat cooking spray for oil. Another common substitution for butter is margarine. Before making this substitution, consider the recipe. If it is a dessert, it's often best to use butter. Margarine may noticeably change the taste or consistency of the food.

Some of the recipes in this book call for milk, yogurt, or feta cheese. You may cut fat by using skim, 1 percent, or 2 percent milk and nonfat or low-fat yogurt instead. You may wish to use a combination of nonfat and whole milk products to achieve the desired flavor with less fat. For a healthier feta cheese dish, substitute low-fat or nonfat varieties.

Meat, such as lamb and beef, play a big part in Turkish cooking. Some cooks like to replace red meat with chicken, turkey, or chunks of tofu to lower the fat content. However, since this does change the flavor, you may need to experiment a little bit to decide if you like these substitutions. Buying extra-lean cuts of lamb or beef or trimming excess fat from the meat is also an easy way to reduce fat.

When recipes call for lamb, beef, or chicken broth, use low-fat varieties or replace with vegetable broth. You may lower the cholesterol in some of the dishes that contain eggs by using an egg substitute.

There are many ways to prepare meals that are good for you and still taste great. As you become a more experienced cook, try experimenting with recipes and substitutions to find the methods that work best.

METRIC CONVERSIONS

Cooks in the United States measure both liquid and solid ingredients using standard containers based on the 8-ounce cup and the tablespoon. These measurements are based on volume, while the metric system of measurement is based on both weight (for solids) and volume (for liquids). To convert from U.S. fluid tablespoons, ounces, quarts, and so forth to metric liters is a straightforward conversion, using the chart below. However, since solids have different weights—one cup of rice does not weigh the same as one cup of grated cheese, for example—many cooks who use the metric system have kitchen scales to weigh different ingredients. The chart below will give you a good starting point for basic conversions to the metric system.

MASS (weight)

1 ounce (oz.)	=	28.0 grams (g)
8 ounces	=	227.0 grams
1 pound (lb.)		
or 16 ounces	=	0.45 kilograms (kg)
2.2 pounds	=	1.0 kilogram

LIQUID VOLUME

1 teaspoon (tsp.)	=	5.0 milliliters (ml)
1 tablespoon (tbsp.)	=	15.0 milliliters
1 fluid ounce (oz.)	=	30.0 milliliters
1 cup (c.)	=	240 milliliters
1 pint (pt.)	=	480 milliliters
1 quart (qt.)	=	0.95 liters (l)
1 gallon (gal.)	=	3.80 liters

LENGTH

¼ inch (in.)	=	0.6 centimeters (cm)
½ inch	=	1.25 centimeters
1 inch	=	2.5 centimeters

TEMPERATURE

212°F	=	100°C (boiling point of water)
225°F	=	110°C
250°F	=	120°C
275°F	=	135°C
300°F	=	150°C
325°F	=	160°C
350°F	=	180°C
375°F	=	190°C
400°F	=	200°C

(To convert temperature in Fahrenheit to Celsius, subtract 32 and multiply by .56)

PAN SIZES

8-inch cake pan	=	20 x 4-centimeter cake pan
9-inch cake pan	=	23 x 3.5-centimeter cake pan
11 x 7-inch baking pan	=	28 x 18-centimeter baking pan
13 x 9-inch baking pan	=	32.5 x 23-centimeter baking pan
9 x 5-inch loaf pan	=	23 x 13-centimeter loaf pan
2-quart casserole	=	2-liter casserole

A Turkish Table

In most Turkish homes and restaurants, diners enjoy their meals while sitting on chairs at a table. It's not uncommon, however, for families in some small villages to eat as the Ottoman Turks did—sitting on cushions or carpets gathered around a low table called a *sofra*. These people either cross their legs or sit with one foot tucked under them with the other foot planted flat on the ground. A tablecloth, or *masa örtüsü*, typically covers the eating area, and diners may drape a section over their laps to use as a napkin. Traditional meals are served from a shared central plate, and diners often scoop food into their mouths with pita bread or spoons.

Whether in a traditional setting or the fanciest restaurant in İstanbul, a basket of fresh-baked crusty bread (*ekmek*) or pita adorns every table. Diners may nibble on bread to ease their hunger as they wait for the main course or use the bread to soak up the remains of a delicious sauce after enjoying the main course. Dining in Turkey is a very social affair. When they have the time, Turks will linger around the dinner table, enjoying good conversation and extra helpings. After dinner, they may continue to talk away from the table while sipping tea or coffee and savoring fresh fruit such as watermelon or strawberries.

A restaurant cook in İstanbul sits on the floor to prepare stuffed pitas in a traditional way.

A Turkish Menu

A typical Turkish day begins with *kahvaltı* (breakfast). On days off, this meal consists of börek, fried eggs with *sucuk* (Turkish sausage) or pastirma, honey, fresh bread, and hot milk. On busier days, Turks may eat a quickly prepared spread with fresh bread, white cheese, honey, or a variety of jams such as rose-petal jam, hard-boiled eggs, olives, fresh tomato and cucumber slices, and tea. Lunch, or *öğle yemeği*, often consists of some of the same foods eaten for breakfast. Between 6 and 9 in the evening, Turks sit down with their families for dinner, or *akşam yemeği*. This meal might begin with red lentil soup, seasoned with fresh lemon juice. Chicken or lamb with rice or bulgur might make up a typical main course, and desserts such as fresh fruits or milky puddings might complete the meal. Below are two typical Turkish dinner menus, one that features meat as its main course and one that is vegetarian.

DINNER #1

Red lentil soup

Lamb kebabs with tomatoes, peppers, and onions

Burnt rice pudding

SHOPPING LIST:

Produce

3 medium onions
1 bulb of garlic
1 lemon
3 red or green bell peppers
1 pint cherry tomatoes

Dairy/Egg/Meat

1 lb. lamb, cut into 1-inch cubes
1 quart milk

Canned/Bottled/Boxed

olive oil
2 quarts low-fat vegetable or beef stock
8-oz. can tomato paste
¼ c. lemon juice
vanilla extract

Miscellaneous

salt
pepper
dried mint
cinnamon
cumin
coriander
1 dried red pepper (optional)
1 c. red lentils
¾ c. short-grain rice
sugar

DINNER #2

Zucchini fritters

Shredded wheat soup
with tomatoes

Eggplant with onion
and tomatoes

Flat bread with nigella
seeds

Baklava

SHOPPING LIST:

Produce

1 large zucchini
1 large and 1 small onion
1 bulb of garlic
1 lemon
2 eggplants
7 tomatoes
1 bunch fresh dill
2 bunches fresh parsley
1 bunch fresh basil
½ c. walnuts, pistachios, or
almonds

Dairy/Egg/Meat

3 eggs
3 tbsp. grated Parmesan
cheese
¾ lb. (3 sticks) butter

Canned/Bottled/Boxed

olive oil
rose water
32 to 40 oz. vegetable stock
vermicelli pasta

Miscellaneous

unbleached, all-purpose flour
salt
pepper
1½ lb. sugar
2 envelopes (4 tsp.) active
dry yeast
bread flour
1 16-oz. package of phyllo
dough
2 tbsp. nigella seeds or
sesame seeds

Appetizers

The Turkish word for appetizers is *meze*, which means "a pleasant taste." An assortment of meze may be served before the main meal as a way to jump-start the taste buds, preparing them for the delicious food to come. Many adults in Turkey have a glass of wine or raki, an anise-flavored liquor, with meze such as smoked eggplant with yogurt, bulgur patties, stuffed grape leaves, or zucchini fritters. In Turkish homes, families might start a meal with a meze.

This section also includes recipes for foods that vendors commonly sell on the streets of İstanbul, Ankara, İzmir, and other Turkish cities and towns. The aroma of roasted corn-on-the-cob, toasted sesame bread rings called *simit*, kebabs, *etli ekmek* (meat pizza), and gözleme tempt passersby and prevent Turks and visitors alike from going hungry between meals.

Try making tasty little pizzas the way Turkish people do. (Recipe on pages 32–33.)

Meat Pizza / Lahmacun

Dough:

½ envelope (1 tsp.) active dry yeast

1 tsp. sugar

2 tbsp. milk

5 c. flour

4 tbsp. butter at room temperature

2 eggs, lightly beaten

1 tsp. salt

Topping:

2 tbsp. olive oil

1 onion, chopped

8 oz. ground lamb

1 handful fresh parsley, chopped

1 egg yolk, separated (the white can
   be thrown away)*

1 tbsp. butter, melted

1. In a small bowl, combine yeast and sugar with milk. Allow to sit for 10 minutes.

2. Pour flour into a large bowl and create a well in center. Pour yeast mixture into well, and add butter and eggs. Stir to combine, and then turn dough out onto a clean floured surface. Use your hands to knead mixture for about 10 minutes, or until a soft dough mixture. Put in a lightly oiled bowl and cover with a damp towel. Set aside and let rise in a warm place for 1 hour.

3. Preheat oven to 450°F. Divide dough into golf ball-sized pieces. On a floured cookie sheet, use your hands to flatten each piece into a circle about ¼-inch thick.

4. In a medium skillet, heat olive oil over medium heat. Add onion and sauté for 5 minutes. Add meat and cook for 5 minutes more, stirring often. Mix in parsley.

5. Spread a layer of topping about ⅛-inch thick in the middle of each piece of dough. Along the outside edge of each pizza, fold ¼ inch of dough toward center to create a border of crust.

6. Leave pizzas in a warm place to rise for another 30 minutes. Use a pastry brush to coat outer crusts with egg yolk (discard egg white). Bake for 5 to 10 minutes, or until golden brown.

7. When cooked, brush lightly with melted butter and stack in a covered saucepan for 5 minutes before serving. (This step is to soften the pastry. If you want a crisp crust, serve straight from the oven.)

*Preparation time: 2 hours***
Cooking time: 10 minutes
Serves 6

*To separate an egg, carefully crack it over a small bowl without breaking the yolk. Pour the yolk from one eggshell half to the other, dropping a little bit of the white into the bowl each time. When only the yolk remains, pour it into a separate dish.

** If you are short on time, try using frozen bread dough instead of making your own.

Zucchini Fritters/Mücver

¼ c. flour

I egg, beaten

3 tbsp. grated Parmesan cheese

I tbsp. fresh dill, chopped

I tbsp. fresh parsley, chopped

½ tsp. salt

¼ tsp. pepper

I c. zucchini, grated

I small onion, grated

¼ c. olive oil for frying

1. In a large bowl, combine flour, egg, cheese, dill, parsley, salt, and pepper. Mix in grated zucchini and onion.

2. In a large skillet, heat oil until very hot, but not smoking.* Drop mixture into hot oil one tablespoonful at a time. Fry each fritter for about 5 minutes on each side, or until it is golden brown. Use a spatula to transfer fritters to a plate lined with paper towels and allow to drain. Serve hot.

Preparation time: 5 minutes
Cooking time: 30 minutes
Serves 6

Cooking with hot oil is simple and safe as long as you're careful and an adult is present. Be sure to use long-handled utensils whenever possible. Stand as far back from the stove as you can while you slowly drop the mixture, one tablespoonful at a time, into oil to avoid splattering.

Spinach-Filled Anatolian Flat Bread/
Ispanakh Gözleme

Dough:

½ c. unbleached flour

½ tsp. salt

1 tbsp. olive oil

¼ c. lukewarm water

Filling:

1 tbsp. olive oil, plus extra for
    coating

1 large onion, chopped

4 cloves garlic, minced

1 c. fresh spinach, washed and
    patted dry*

1 pinch nutmeg

¼ tsp. pepper

1 tbsp. feta cheese

3 tbsp. grated Parmesan cheese

1 tbsp. flour

½ c. milk

1. In a large bowl, combine flour and salt. Create a well in the center and add 1 tablespoon oil and water. Use your hands to work liquid ingredients into flour and salt. Knead in bowl for 10 minutes.

2. Divide dough into four balls and place them on a floured surface. Cover with a damp cloth and let rest for 25 minutes.

3. Meanwhile, prepare filling. Heat 1 tablespoon olive oil in a medium saucepan over medium heat. Add onion and garlic and sauté until soft and translucent (clear), about 5 to 10 minutes.

4. Add spinach, nutmeg, pepper, feta cheese, and Parmesan cheese and cover with a lid. Cook for about 3 minutes.

5. Mix flour and milk in a small bowl. Add to spinach mixture, stirring constantly to create a thick sauce. Remove pan from heat.

6. Use a rolling pin to roll balls, one by one, into circles between 5 and 6 inches in diameter and ¼-inch thick.

7. Divide spinach mixture into four even parts. Spread mixture over the middle of each circle of dough, leaving about 1 inch of space between the spinach mixture and the edge of the dough. Fold edges of dough inward so that the edges meet in the center and cover the filling.

8. Warm a large nonstick skillet over medium heat and place one of the folded circles of dough in pan.

9. Carefully use a spatula to push dough around in pan, making sure that it browns evenly on the bottom and doesn't stick. Cook for about 2 minutes.

10. Use a pastry brush to apply a thin coat of olive oil to the uncooked side of the dough. Flip flat bread with a spatula and cook for another 2 minutes. Move finished bread to a dish and cover to keep warm. Repeat with remaining dough.

Preparation time: 45 minutes**
Cooking time: 25 minutes
Serves 4

* Try using different fillings such as cooked shredded chicken or cooked shredded lamb with cheese. Make a dessert gözleme by using honey and mashed bananas, or just a sprinkling of chocolate chips.

** If you are short on time, try using frozen bread dough instead of making your own.

Soups and Side Dishes

In Turkey, soups and side dishes provide nourishment any time of the day, including at breakfast. During Ramazan, for example, Turkish Muslims will often eat soup during the predawn meal to give them energy for the long hours of fasting ahead. Soup is so popular in Turkey that soup houses, which tend to specialize in a particular kind of soup, sell heaping bowls of soup all day and late into the night. The two soups included in this section are flavorful and easy to make. Serve small amounts of soup before a main course to trigger the appetite. You can also serve side dishes or large bowlfuls of soup with bread on the side to create a complete lunch or dinner.

A satisfying vegetarian meal might start with shredded wheat soup with tomatoes. (Recipe on page 41.)

Red Lentil Soup/ Kırmızı Mercimek Çorbası

1 tbsp. butter or olive oil

1 onion, chopped

2 cloves garlic, minced

1 tsp. ground cumin

1 tsp. ground coriander

2 tbsp. tomato paste

8 c. low-fat vegetable or beef stock

1 c. red lentils

¼ c. short-grain rice

1 dried red pepper (optional)

½ tsp. salt

¼ tsp. pepper

½ tsp. dried mint

1 lemon, cut into wedges

1. In a Dutch oven, warm butter or olive oil over medium heat.

2. Add onion and sauté for 5 to 10 minutes, or until onion is translucent.

3. Stir in garlic, cumin, and coriander, and cook for 1 to 2 minutes.

4. Add tomato paste, stock, lentils, rice, and red pepper (if desired). Stir to combine.

5. Bring soup to a boil, cover pan, and reduce heat to a simmer.

6. Cook for about 30 to 40 minutes, stirring occasionally.

7. When lentils and rice are tender and soup has thickened, add salt, pepper, and dried mint. Serve hot with lemon wedges.

Preparation time: 5 minutes
Cooking time: 1 hour
Serves 4

Shredded Wheat Soup with Tomatoes/
Domatesli Tel Şerhriye Çorbası

3 ripe tomatoes, peeled and coarsely chopped*

1 c. water

4 to 5 c. canned vegetable stock

½ c. vermicelli pasta, broken into ½-inch pieces

½ tsp. salt

¼ tsp. black pepper

2 tbsp. butter, melted

1 handful fresh parsley, chopped

1. In a large saucepan, combine tomatoes and water. Bring to a boil over high heat. Boil for 10 minutes longer. Over a medium bowl, pour tomatoes and water through a strainer, using a spoon to press as much of tomato mixture through as possible. Discard pulp and set aside juice.

2. In a Dutch oven, bring stock to a boil and add vermicelli.

3. Add reserved tomato juice to Dutch oven, add salt and pepper, and simmer for about 8 minutes, or until vermicelli is tender.

4. Combine melted butter and parsley. Add to soup and serve.

Preparation time: 15 minutes
Cooking time: 30 minutes
Serves 4

To peel a tomato, place it in a small saucepan of boiling water for about 1 minute. Remove with a slotted spoon and cool until the tomato is warm but no longer hot. Use a small paring knife to peel off the skin. It will come off easily.

Green Beans with Minced Meat/Etli Taze Fasulye

1½ tbsp. olive oil

2 onions, chopped

8 oz. (½ lb.) cubed lamb*

2 tomatoes, peeled and chopped, or
    1 tbsp. tomato paste

3 c. plus 2 c. hot water

4 lb. fresh green beans, ends
    removed and sliced in half

½ green bell pepper, seeded and
    chopped

½ tsp. salt

1. In a medium skillet, heat olive oil over medium heat. Sauté onions until slightly brown on edges. Add cubed meat and cook for 7 to 10 minutes longer.

2. Add tomatoes or tomato paste and 3 cups hot water. Lower heat to a simmer. Cook until meat is tender, or about 30 minutes.

3. Stir in beans and green pepper and cook for 10 minutes over medium heat.

4. Add 2 cups of hot water and simmer until vegetables are tender, or about 5 minutes.

5. Add salt to taste. Serve with rice.

Preparation time: 10 minutes
Cooking time: 1 hour
Serves 4

*To make this a vegetarian dish, simply
omit the lamb.*

Main Dishes

The main course at a traditional Turkish feast almost always consists of meat. Most often the meat course is *şiş kebab* (lamb that has been cut into cubes, skewered, and grilled). Flavors and preparation techniques vary from region to region. The most common kebab consists of alternating putting cubes of meat and chunks of fresh vegetables on a skewer. But all-meat kebabs are another option, and some cooks use different kinds of ground meats, mixed with a variety of spices, and shaped by hand. And if you don't eat meat, make a kebab using fresh vegetables such as wedges of green or red bell peppers, onions, zucchini, eggplant, whole mushrooms, or cherry tomatoes.

Chicken cooked with rice, tomatoes, red or green bell peppers, and tarragon is another appetizing main course from Turkey. (Recipe on pages 46–47.)

Chicken with Rice, Tomatoes, Peppers, and Tarragon/*Domatesli Pirinçli Piliç*

- 3 tbsp. olive oil
- 2 large onions, chopped fine
- 1 whole chicken, in pieces*
- 2 red or green bell peppers, seeded and chopped
- 1 or 2 jalapeño peppers, chopped fine**
- 3 tbsp. fresh tarragon, chopped
- 2 medium tomatoes, peeled and chopped (see recipe on p. 41 for peeling instructions)
- ½ tsp. salt
- ½ tsp. black pepper
- 3 8-oz. cans low-fat chicken stock
- 2 c. short-grain rice, rinsed and drained

1. Heat olive oil in a large skillet and sauté onions for about 10 minutes, or until lightly browned. Using a slotted spoon, transfer onions to a small bowl and set aside.

2. Add chicken pieces to skillet and cook over medium heat, turning until golden brown on all sides. Push chicken to one side of pan and add bell peppers, jalapeños, and tarragon.

3. Sauté for 1 minute. Add tomatoes, browned onions, salt, and pepper. Stir to combine sauce with chicken pieces. Cover and simmer for 20 minutes.

4. Meanwhile, in a separate saucepan, heat chicken stock.

5. Transfer chicken to a clean plate and set aside. (Leave tomato mixture in skillet.)

6. Add rice to tomato mixture and stir until thoroughly combined. Add warmed chicken stock to tomato and rice mixture. Raise heat to high and boil for 1 minute.

7. Add remaining chicken pieces to pan. Cover, reduce heat, and simmer for 15 minutes, or until all of liquid is absorbed.

8. Remove pan from heat, cover and let sit for 10 minutes.

9. Stir and serve hot.

Preparation time: 15 minutes
Cooking time: 1 hour
Serves 4 to 6

After handling raw chicken or other poultry, always remember to thoroughly wash your hands, utensils, and preparation area with hot, soapy water. Also, when checking chicken for doneness, it's a good idea to cut it open gently to make sure the meat is white (not pink) all the way through.

**Be careful when working with hot peppers. The oil on the skin of the peppers can burn you, so wear rubber gloves while cutting the pepper, and be sure to remove all the seeds. Wash your hands well when you are done.*

Dumplings with Yogurt/Mantı

7 oz. ground lamb or beef

3 medium onions, chopped

½ tsp. salt

½ tsp. pepper

I package wonton wrappers*

6 c. water or vegetable stock

¼ c. butter

I tsp. paprika

1¾ c. plain yogurt

*Wonton wrappers are small, thin squares or rounds of soft dough made from flour, water, and eggs.

1. Preheat oven to 350°F. In a large bowl, combine meat, onion, salt, and pepper.

2. Arrange wonton wrappers on a clean surface. Place ½ teaspoon of filling in the center of each wonton wrapper. Pull the corners of each square toward the center to cover meat. Pinch corners together to form a bundle.

3. Transfer dumplings to a lightly buttered 11×7-inch baking dish. Bake for 25 minutes, or until golden brown.

4. Meanwhile, boil water or stock. Carefully take baking dish from oven and pour liquid over dumplings. Cover dish with foil. Bake for about 1 hour, or until most of water has been absorbed and dumplings are soft. Drain remaining water.

5. Melt butter and pour half over top of dumplings. Add paprika to remaining butter. Set aside.

6. In a small bowl, beat yogurt with a fork until it is thin and creamy and pour it over dumplings. Just before serving, pour melted butter with paprika over top. Serve warm.

Preparation time: 30 minutes
Cooking time: 1½ hours
Serves 6 to 8

Lamb Kebabs with Tomatoes, Peppers, and Onions/
Şiş Kebap

This classic Turkish dish is delicious and easy to make. You can cook the kebabs on a grill or place them on a broiler pan and broil in the oven.

Marinade for lamb:

2 medium onions, chopped

2 cloves garlic

¼ c. lemon juice

2 tsp. salt

I tsp. cumin

I tbsp. olive oil

Kebab pieces:

I lb. lean lamb, cut into I-inch
  cubes*

I pint cherry tomatoes

3 red or green bell peppers, seeded
  and chopped into quarters

*Chicken or beef can be used in place of lamb. Or, to make this a vegetarian dish, use cubed eggplant instead.

**If using wooden skewers, be sure to soak them in water for about 30 minutes before using.

1. To make marinade, put chopped onions, crushed garlic, lemon juice, salt, cumin, and olive oil into a food processor and puree.

2. Transfer mixture to a bowl and add lamb pieces. Stir to combine, cover with plastic wrap, and refrigerate for at least 6 hours.

3. If grilling kebabs, ask an adult to light the grill about 45 minutes before you are ready to cook, or to preheat the broiler about 5 minutes beforehand.

4. Thread lamb pieces, tomatoes, and pepper chunks onto skewers,** alternating ingredients.

5. Grill or broil for 6 minutes on each side.

6. Use a fork to slide cooked lamb and vegetable pieces from skewers onto a plate. Serve with yogurt and flat bread.

Preparation time: 10 minutes
(plus 6 hours marinating time)
Cooking time: 12 minutes
Serves 4

Eggplant with Onion and Tomatoes/İmam Bayıldı

The Turkish name for this dish means "The Imam Swooned," and that is just what an imam, a religious leader, did when he first tasted this delightful concoction.

2 medium eggplants

1 tsp. salt

1 large onion, finely chopped

4 medium tomatoes, peeled and chopped (see recipe on p. 41 for peeling instructions)

6 cloves garlic, minced

½ c. fresh parsley, chopped

¼ c. fresh dill, chopped

¼ c. fresh basil, chopped

½ c. olive oil

¼ c. water

1 tbsp. sugar

1 lemon, cut into wedges

1. Preheat oven to 350°F. Wash each eggplant, cut off tops, and slice in half lengthwise. Arrange halves in a medium-sized roasting pan, flesh side up.

2. In a large bowl, combine salt with onion, tomatoes, garlic, parsley, dill, and basil. Stir in 2 tablespoons of oil. Spoon mixture over eggplant halves, piling as much on top of them as possible.

3. Combine remaining olive oil with water and sugar in same bowl. Pour over eggplant halves.

4. Bake in oven for 1½ hours, pressing tomato mixture into eggplant flesh once or twice as eggplant halves bake. Eggplant is ready when it is very soft.

5. Remove from oven and transfer eggplant halves to a serving dish. Pour oil mixture from bottom of pan over eggplant halves. Serve with lemon slices.

Preparation time: 15 minutes
Cooking time: 1½ hours
Serves 4

Desserts

Dessert in Turkey usually consists of a platter filled with seasonal fresh fruits set in the center of the table. In the summertime, red, ripe strawberries are popular. In August and September, fresh watermelon is a sweet, refreshing way to complete a meal. But on special occasions, Turkish cooks may buy baklava or other pastries from the local bakery or stop by the nearest sweet shop to select a favorite flavor of Turkish delight. Or, if they have the time, they may make a pudding such as burnt rice pudding or almond cream. Diners usually linger over dessert, talking and drinking cup after cup of sweet, black tea.

Traditional Turkish baklava is a dessert that stands out on any table. (Recipe on pages 54–55.)

Baklava

It was once common for grandmothers to make baklava from scratch, rolling out very thin layers of dough to assemble the pastry. However, modern cooks in Turkey usually buy this classic
dessert or snack from the bakery. This recipe, which uses ready-made phyllo dough, is relatively
easy to make. A day before making baklava, move the frozen phyllo dough to the refrigerator to
give it plenty of time to thaw completely.

Syrup:

1 c. water

1 lb. sugar

1 tbsp. rose water

Pastry:

olive oil to brush on sheet of
    aluminum foil in baking dish

1 16-oz. package phyllo dough,
    thawed*

1 c. butter (2 sticks), melted

¼ c. plus ¼ c. walnuts, pistachios,
    or almonds, chopped fine

1. Preheat oven to 400°F.

2. To make syrup, combine water and
   sugar in a saucepan and bring to a
   boil. Reduce heat and simmer for
   10 minutes. Add rose water, stir,
   and set aside.

3. Line a square baking dish (9×9)
   with a sheet of aluminum foil. Use
   a pastry brush to apply olive oil to
   foil lining. Lay one sheet of phyllo
   dough on top of foil and brush it
   with a thin coating of melted
   butter.**

4. Add next layer of phyllo dough.
   Continue adding layers and
   brushing each with butter until
   you've assembled five layers.

5. Sprinkle fifth layer with ¼ cup
   chopped nuts.

6. Add five more layers of phyllo,
   brushing each with butter.

7. Sprinkle tenth layer with remaining
   nuts.

8. Add five more layers of phyllo dough, brushing each with butter.

9. Use a sharp knife to cut baklava into 1-inch squares. Trim any excess dough that may overlap sides of pan.

10. Bake baklava for 30 to 40 minutes, or until top is golden brown.

11. Remove from oven and brush top with butter.

12. Slowly pour rose water syrup evenly over squares. Allow to cool before serving. Store leftover baklava at room temperature.

Preparation time: 20 minutes
Cooking time: 15 minutes
Baking time: 40 minutes
Serves 8

*Thaw frozen phyllo dough in its original package for 24 hours in the refrigerator. Do not unwrap phyllo until you are ready to use it. Make sure your work area is cleared, your melted butter and pastry brush are ready, and your filling is prepared.

**After removing a sheet of phyllo from the package, cover remaining sheets tightly with either plastic wrap or a slightly damp kitchen towel (not terry cloth). Leftover phyllo will stay fresh in the refrigerator for one week if covered well with plastic wrap.

Burnt Rice Pudding / Sütlâç

1¾ c. water

½ c. uncooked short-grain rice

4 c. milk

1 c. sugar

⅛ c. rice flour

2 tsp. vanilla extract

1 tsp. cinnamon

1. In a small saucepan, bring water to a boil. Stir in rice, cover pan, and lower heat to a simmer. Cook for 20 to 30 minutes, or until almost all water is absorbed.

2. Meanwhile, combine milk and sugar in a medium saucepan. Cook over low heat and stir until sugar dissolves.

3. In a small bowl, combine rice flour with 2 or 3 tablespoons of the warm milk, stirring to make a thick paste.

4. Add cooked rice to warmed milk and bring to a boil over medium heat.

5. Add rice flour paste to rice and milk mixture, stirring constantly.

6. Lower heat to a simmer and cook for 20 minutes, stirring often.

7. Turn off heat and stir in vanilla. Divide pudding into four ovenproof serving bowls and sprinkle with cinnamon.

8. Preheat broiler for 5 minutes.

9. Broil bowls of pudding for 5 to 10 minutes, or until browned on top. Serve warm.

Preparation time: 10 minutes
Cooking time: 1 to 1¼ hour
Serves 4

Almond Cream / Keşkül

½ c. blanched almonds

2 c. milk

⅛ c. rice flour

½ c. sugar

1 tbsp. coconut

1 tbsp. finely chopped pistachios

1. In a food processor or blender, grind almonds until fine. Add 2 tablespoons of milk and blend to a smooth paste.

2. In a small bowl, combine rice flour with 1 tablespoon of milk and stir to a pastelike consistency.

3. Pour remaining milk and sugar into a saucepan and bring to a boil, stirring constantly.

4. Turn heat down to a simmer. Add 2 to 3 tablespoons of hot milk to rice flour mixture and mix well. Scrape all of the rice flour mixture into the milk in saucepan, stirring to combine.

5. Add almond paste to saucepan and stir constantly. Simmer for about 30 minutes, stirring occasionally, until mixture thickens.

6. Divide into individual dessert dishes, garnish with coconut and pistachios, and chill for at least 1 hour before serving.

Preparation time: 10 minutes
(plus 1 hour chilling time)
Cooking time: 40 minutes
Serves 4

Turkish Delight/ *Lokum*

Although Turks tend to buy this traditional treat at candy shops, it can be fun to make it yourself. Be careful, however, when you make this recipe—sugar water burns easily.

2 tbsp. plus ¼ c. cornstarch

2 tbsp. plus 2 c. water

2 tbsp. rose water**

2¼ c. granulated sugar

⅛ c. plus ⅛ c. powdered sugar

1. Line an 8-inch cake pan with a layer of cheesecloth.* Sprinkle with 2 tablespoons cornstarch, creating a thin layer.

2. Pour remaining cornstarch into a small bowl. Mix in 2 tablespoons water to make a paste. Stir in rose water.

3. In a small saucepan, make a sugar syrup by combining sugar and 2 cups water. Bring to a boil, stirring constantly until sugar is completely dissolved. Cook without stirring for about 5 minutes more.

4. Add 2 tablespoons of the sugar syrup to the cornstarch mixture and stir to combine.

5. Add cornstarch mixture to saucepan with sugar syrup and stir constantly over medium heat until mixture thickens. Mixture is ready when a bit of it dropped into a glass of cold water forms into a soft ball (240°F on a candy thermometer).

6. Pour mixture into prepared cake pan, scraping sides of sauce pan to remove all of syrup. Allow mixture to cool.

7. Dust a clean cutting board with $\frac{1}{8}$-cup powdered sugar and turn Turkish delight onto it. Peel off cheesecloth and brush off any extra cornstarch.

8. Cut Turkish delight into 1-inch squares.

9. Return squares to cake pan. Sprinkle remaining powdered sugar over squares in cake pan. Lightly shake pan back and forth to coat all sides of squares in sugar. Store in a tightly sealed container for up to 6 months.

Preparation time: 15 minutes
Cooking time: 30 minutes plus cooling time
Makes 25 pieces

*Cheesecloth is a gauzy cotton cloth that can be used as a strainer. It is available at most grocery stores or at specialty cooking shops.

**Turkish delight is also very good with nuts. Try omitting the rose water and adding shelled, chopped pistachios instead.

Holiday and Festival Food

In a country of people who love to eat, holidays and other celebrations revolve around good food that is painstakingly prepared. Many of the recipes included in this section are only made on special occasions. Güllaç is usually served only during Ramazan. Börek dishes typically appear on the table during holidays or other festive celebrations. *Tepsi böreği*, the börek recipe included in this section, might be served during Ramazan, Kurban Bayramı, or at a wedding feast.

One holiday, Aşure Bayramı, is all about the food for which it is named. *Aşure* is a pudding of cereal grains, sugar, and raisins. During the month that follows the feast of sacrifice (Kurban Bayramı), women in almost every household prepare this dessert in large amounts, offering it to guests and sending it to relatives and neighbors. And, because everyone makes it, families and friends usually just end up exchanging bowls of the sweet dish!

Tradition has it that aşure was invented after a great flood that, according to a Biblical story, covered the world. Noah built an ark (ship) in anticipation of the flood. When the flood subsided, the ark carrying Noah's group of survivors came to rest on Mount Ararat in northeastern Turkey. Noah called for a celebration. Although the passengers' supplies were nearly exhausted, they used what food remained to make a splendid feast of aşure. The aşure recipe we've included in this section, Noah's Dessert, is a great rainy-day activity.

For a holiday meal, dress up an ordinary flat bread by coating it with sesame or nigella seeds. (Recipe on pages 64-65.)

Flat Bread with Nigella Seeds/*Pita*

Flat bread is a Turkish staple that is popular throughout the year. After fasting all day during Ramazan, however, this bread is especially welcomed. The sprinkling of nigella seeds across the bread's crusty top gives it a special touch during holiday feasts.

2 envelopes (4 tsp.) active dry yeast

½ tsp. sugar

½ c. plus 1 c. lukewarm water

½ c. unbleached, all-purpose flour

3½ c. bread flour

1 tsp. salt

3 tbsp. olive oil, plus additional for coating

2 eggs, lightly beaten

2 tbsp. nigella seeds or sesame seeds

1. In a medium bowl, dissolve yeast and sugar in ½ cup lukewarm water. Set aside in a warm place for 10 minutes, until mixture is frothy. Add all-purpose flour and stir until well combined. Cover with plastic wrap and let rise for 30 minutes.

2. Pour bread flour into a large bowl and create a well in center. Add yeast mixture, salt, 3 tablespoons olive oil, and 1 cup lukewarm water. Use your hands to gradually combine flour with remaining ingredients, creating a sticky dough.

3. Turn dough out onto a clean floured surface and knead for about 15 minutes. As you work dough, it will become less sticky but should remain moist and easy to work with.

4. Coat a medium bowl with a very thin layer of olive oil. Place dough in bowl and cover with plastic wrap. Let dough rise for 1 hour, until almost doubled in size.

5. Divide dough into two balls and place on a cookie sheet. Cover with a clean, damp kitchen towel and let rise for 30 minutes longer.

6. Preheat oven to 450°F and place an empty cookie sheet in warm oven.

7. Flatten one ball of dough into a disk, stretching it into a 10-inch circle about ¼-inch thick. Use your thumb and forefinger to pinch a ½-inch-thick rim about 1 inch in from edge, all the way around. Use your fingertips to make shallow indentations all over the surface of dough. Repeat with other ball.

8. Using an oven mitt, remove cookie sheet from oven. Carefully place flat bread on sheet. Brush tops with beaten egg and sprinkle with nigella or sesame seeds. Bake for 10 to 15 minutes, or until bread is golden with crusty edges. Serve fresh from oven.

Preparation time: 2 hours, 15 minutes
Baking time: 15 minutes
Makes two 10-inch round loaves

Noah's Dessert / Aşure

½ c. barley, soaked in 3 c. water 6 hours or overnight

4 c. water

¼ c. raisins

¼ c. dried apricots chopped fine

¼ c. currants, plus 1 tbsp. for garnish

¼ c. short-grain rice

¼ tsp. salt

½ c. canned chickpeas, rinsed and drained

½ c. canned kidney beans, rinsed and drained

2 tbsp. cornstarch, mixed with 2 tsp. milk

½ c. sugar

1 tbsp. rose water

¼ c. dried figs, chopped fine

3 tbsp. chopped almonds

3 tbsp. chopped walnuts

1 tbsp. pine nuts

1. Soak raisins, apricots, and currants in very hot water for 5 minutes. Drain.

2. Drain soaked barley and transfer to large saucepan. Add 4 cups water to barley and bring to a boil. Cover, reduce heat, and simmer for 25 minutes, or until tender.

3. Add rice. Cook for 10 minutes more.

4. Stir in salt, chickpeas, kidney beans, raisins, apricots, and ¼ cup currants. Cook over medium heat for 10 minutes.

5. Meanwhile, combine cornstarch mixture with 2 tablespoons of cooking liquid in a small bowl. Set aside.

6. Add sugar to barley mixture. Stir for 2 minutes. Add cornstarch mixture and stir until mixture thickens.

8. Return mixture to a boil. Add rose water and simmer for 10 minutes.

9. Transfer pudding to a serving bowl. Refrigerate and serve cold, garnished with currants, figs, almonds, walnuts, and pine nuts.

Preparation time: 30 minutes
(plus at least 6 hours soaking time)
Cooking time: 1 hour
Serves 6

Baked Meat and Cheese Pie / Tepsi Böreği

This very popular dish is cooked in a variety of ways using different ingredients. It can be made with cheese, potatoes, vegetables, meat or a combination of these ingredients. It can be cooked in oil, fried, or baked. No matter what, it's always delicious.

1 tbsp. butter

1 large onion, chopped fine

3 cloves garlic, minced and mixed with ¼ tsp. salt

8 oz. ground beef or lamb*

1 tsp. cinnamon

3 tbsp. fresh parsley, chopped

2 tbsp. fresh dill, chopped

½ tsp. salt

½ tsp. fresh ground pepper

2 eggs

1 c. milk

½ c. olive oil

1 16 oz. package phyllo dough, thawed**

*To make this a vegetarian dish, omit the lamb, cinnamon, and herbs and add 3 cups fresh spinach, 1 tablespoon feta cheese, 1 pinch grated nutmeg, and 3 tablespoon grated Parmesan cheese.

1. Preheat oven to 400°F.

2. In a large skillet, heat butter over medium heat. Add onion, garlic, and salt. Sauté for about 7 minutes, or until onions are soft and translucent.

3. Add meat and stir, cooking for just under 5 minutes.

4. Mix in cinnamon, parsley, dill, salt, and pepper. Remove from heat.

5. In a small bowl, beat eggs with milk and oil.

6. Lightly butter a 9×12-inch baking dish. Carefully press one sheet of phyllo into bottom of pan. (The sheet will overlap the sides of the dish.) Pour a small amount of milk mixture onto phyllo, tilting pan from side to side to moisten dough. Add four more layers of phyllo, brushing each one with milk mixture before adding next one.

7. Add another sheet of phyllo and cover with half meat mixture. Then add four more sheets, again brushing each one with milk mixture.

8. Add another sheet of phyllo dough and cover with remaining meat. Top with five more sheets of phyllo, brushing each with milk mixture.

9. Fold edges of phyllo dough into pan. Brush top thoroughly with milk and egg mixture.

10. Bake for 45 minutes, or until pie is puffy and golden brown. Serve hot or cold.

Preparation time: 45 minutes
Baking time: 45 minutes
Serves 6

**See page 55 for tips on thawing phyllo and handling individual sheets of it.

Index

About the Authors

Kari Cornell is an avid cook who loves to experiment with new recipes and cuisines. As an editor and co-author of children's books for the past six years, Kari is pleased to be able to combine the two activities she enjoys most to write *Cooking the Turkish Way*.

Nurçay Türkoğlu is a professor of Communications at Marmara University in İstanbul, Turkey, who believes that any attempt to understand a culture requires a close look at its food. Nurçay is happy to be able to contribute some childhood memories and recipes to this book, with warm thanks to her mother.

Photo Acknowledgments
The photographs in this book are reproduced with the permission of: © Kari Cornell, pp. 2–3; © Walter and Louiseann Pietrowicz/September 8th Stock, pp. 4 (both), 5 (both), 6, 18, 30, 35, 38, 43, 44, 49, 52, 56, 59, 62, 67; © Jan Butchofsky-Houser/CORBIS, p. 11; © AFP/CORBIS, p. 15; © Hans Georg Roth/CORBIS, p. 17; © Douglas Mesney/CORBIS, p. 26.

Cover photos (front, back, and spine): © Walter and Louiseann Pietrowicz/September 8th Stock.

The illustrations on pages 7, 19, 27, 31, 33, 34, 37, 39, 42, 45, 47, 48, 50, 53, 55, 61, 63, and 68 are by Tim Seeley. The map on page 8 is by Bill Hauser and Cynthia Dahle.